How To Build Your Own Horse Jun

By

Lisa Goodwin

Copyright © 2013 by Lisa Goodwin

Cover design by Lisa Goodwin

All Images throughout this book are by Lisa Goodwin

Printed in the United States of America

ISBN-13: 978-1481932370
ISBN-10: 1481932373

How To Build Your Own Horse Jumps

By

Lisa Goodwin

Table of Contents

DEDICATION

This book is dedicated to horse enthusiasts that are always looking for ways to save money, while never sacrificing the care for the horses they love, and always putting their horses first.

Chapter 1

Why I Wrote This Book

I remember driving down a quiet country road and seeing a beautiful boarding facility. The landscaping was immaculate. My eyes tried to absorb the perfection while I was driving, taking in everything I could and wishing my own stable at home could look like this. Then my eye was drawn to the back of their massive barn. I could see the jumps set up, and it was awesome. Everything was so perfect from the ground, to the jumps. I wanted to have my horse at this barn. At that moment, I decided I wanted my own riding area to look like that.

When I got home, I started searching the internet for horse jumps. The market isn't completely saturated, there were maybe twenty or thirty companies that I could find that specialize in building 'professional' horse jumps. This must be why they are so expensive. I think my eyes bugged out of their sockets when I saw the prices. One company wanted over one thousand dollars, for three jump standards, four poles, and six jump cups!

"What?!?!?!?"

How is this possible I wondered? Why is it so expensive to buy horse jumps? It's just wood and some paint, right? Are they lined with precious metals? And, that price did not even include the shipping! If I wanted to be able to afford a complete set of "professional quality jumps, it would cost me roughly five thousand dollars, before shipping. I don't know about you, but I don't have five thousand dollars to spend on eight jumps that I use maybe three times a week, it doesn't make sense.

So I started playing with making some jumps. The first ones were not what I had envisioned for professional jumps, but they worked. And as my obsession grew, my skill improved, and so did my jumps. Over the next several years I worked on improving my jump building, and even began selling some of my jumps locally, to help offset the cost of my preoccupation of improving my jump building skills.

My jumps may not be fancy, but they are functional. They work well, are sturdy and safe. I made the jumps in the picture above for about two hundred dollars. That includes the paint, jump cups, flower boxes, rails and standards. Five jumps for around two hundred dollars!

Which is why I wrote this book. I don't believe I am the only horse owner who enjoys jumping, nor do I believe I am the only one who thinks that horse jumps are extremely overpriced. In this book I will show you how to make a horse jump complete with rails and jump cups for less than twenty five dollars. I will also focus on just the jump standards. You can make a pair of schooling, or 'stick' standards for less than fifteen dollars. How about creating a pair of wing standards for fifty dollars? I will show you how to make each of these items in this book!

Each chapter is complete with pictures, a materials list and step-by-step instructions on how to build each element of a horse jump. I hope you enjoy it, and more importantly, I hope you will save a lot of money on your horse jumps!

I have five reasons why you should make your own jumps, regardless of the style of riding you do.

1. Variety

By having a few jumps in your riding area, you are varying the same old routine you and your horse are doing day in and day out. Set up four jumps nine feet apart and you have a gymnastic. Set up your jumps in an 'X' and you have a way to practice perfect circles. Line up five jumps in a row, with eight feet in between and you can work on changes of direction. By changing things up for your horse, you will keep him engaged in your training sessions, and variety is good for horses. Change is a good thing when it comes to your riding routine. Good for your horse, and good for you too.

2. Respect

By having jumps that are made of wood, they are substantial. Even having a set of jumps eight inches off the ground, your horse will learn to pick up his feet. It doesn't feel good to hit heavy wood with his hoof, and he will learn to pick up his feet while he is traveling. This may in turn help him to watch where he is going, and round out using his back more, which in turn will help to engage his hindquarters. I'm not a horse trainer, I am only speaking from personal experience of using my jumps for my own horse.

3. Individuality

By creating your own jumps, you can make them whatever you want them to be. You can choose what colors to paint them, where to put them, and how to use them. If you like brown and orange jumps to match your barn, go for it! You will only be limited by your imagination.

Not only can you create what you want, but by experimenting with different jumps, you will help your jumping skills tremendously when you get to the horse show. By changing your jumping elements frequently, you will desensitize your horse to the different types of jumps he will encounter at the horse show.

4. Cost

This is by far the best reason. I am sure you have researched the cost of buying a complete course of jumps, and then seeing the price, opted for maybe just one or two 'professional' jumps, and then said forget it. They are too expensive, and for less than one-tenth of the cost of a professionally built jump course, you can make your own. The most expensive part of your jumps will be the jump cups, which I haven't found an alternative to these, yet. So if the most expensive part of your jump is six dollars a pair, you have just saved a ton of money.

5. Potential income

So now that you have learned how to make your own jumps, why not offer some up for sale? There are so many potential avenues for making a little extra money. There is eBay, Craigslist, flea markets, tack consignments, and the list could go on and on. With a little bit of work, you can make money doing this. Probably not enough to quit your day job, but if done correctly, you could not only make a little extra money, but buy selling some jumps, it could pay for the jumps you made for yourself!

Think about it, if you were to purchase one pair of stick, schooling style jump standards from a jump company how much would it cost? The least expensive pair I have been able to find is on eBay, and they were ninety dollars before the shipping. If you built one pair of regular schooling standards, as I will show you, it will cost roughly ten dollars, I'm not kidding. Ten dollars! That's it! And what is fun about this version of jump standard is that it is unique, and can be customized in many different ways, as I will show you. If you sell one pair of jump standards for fifty dollars, you will not only pay for three of your own jump standards, but this book as well.

With my years of practice and trying to create jumps that were not only functional, but can stand up to the professional version, I have learned many little tips. You will notice throughout this book I will give pointers that really mean to say, *"Trust me, I've done it that way, it didn't turn out so good."* However, with about three hundred jumps worth of 'practice' I feel confident in my abilities, and with all of that practice I am ready to share what I have learned, and you won't have to make the same mistakes that I did.

Although these jumps are homemade, they are no less functional than the professional jumps you may be debating at this moment of purchasing. By paying attention to the small details, you can create professional quality jumps at a fraction of the cost it would be if you were to purchase them.

When building your jumps, there are even more ways to save money than what I have listed throughout this book. Sometimes you can find wood for free on local websites. You can get bargains on paint at home improvement stores, often referred to as 'oops' paint. If you live in an area where there is beetle kill from pine trees, sometimes you can poles for very cheap. There is no right or wrong way when it comes to getting your materials. You can go cheap, or expensive, that is up to you.

I would highly recommend that when you are building your jumps, photograph your progress. It is helpful to have pictures to see where you have come from when building your jumps, and if you are selling them, you will have a great portfolio of what you have been able to create.

All of the pictures that are in this book are jumps that I have created in my spare time, with the tools that I will list for you. These jumps are easy to build, for personal use, and profit. If you follow my directions, you can create beautiful jumps that you will be proud to say, "Yes, I made those!"

Your jumps will get better and better with practice. In no time you will be creating beautiful, professional looking jumps that you will be proud of having.

Chapter 2

The Tools

First things first, you will need tools to create your jumps. The tools are not included in the cost of creating these jumps, but most people have these tools in their garages. If you don't then you will have to purchase them. Don't fret however, these tools will pay for themselves many times over, even if you just use them to make a set of jumps! This may seem like a basic list that anyone should know about, and in most cases this is probably true. However, when I began building jumps I wasted a lot of time searching for these simple items.

1. 18 Volt Drill

The drill is crucial for screwing and drilling holes into your jump standards. I use the rechargeable kind, which allows me to swap out the batteries when one has been exhausted. I have four batteries, because all of my power tools use them interchangeably.

It is also helpful to have a large assortment of different attachments, drill bits, and screwdriver attachments, because you will be interchanging them frequently when making your jumps.

2. Circulating Saw

Although all of my tools are extremely helpful and necessary when it comes to building my jumps, this is the one that is most valuable to me. I am able to make fast work of 4x4's, and all other types of wood because of this saw. It helps to have a backup blade, because the sharper the blade, the faster it cuts through the wood. And if you are using treated lumber, a sharp blade in needed. I actually have two different circular saws. One is an electric one, and it uses a 7 1/4" blade. This is a fantastic saw for doing the major big cuts through thick wood. The other saw is a rechargeable 5" blade circular saw. This one is nice for the smaller cuts where I really need to get in small cuts, such as the little triangle piece that comes off the feet of the jump stamndards.

3. Power Sander

Even though this isn't a necessity, it sure makes sanding a lot faster. You can make fast work of a jump standard with a power sander. I use the triangle, mouse, head type. It makes it easier to get into the nooks and crannies of the corners of the wood.

I have an assortment of sandpapers, depending on how much sanding I need to do. I like the hook and loop style of backing, because that is what my sander is. It's easy and pretty much "Lisa Proof". I say this because if I can do something backwards, or wrong, I usually will.

4. Dremel

Again, not a necessity, it is great for sanding down the holes that have been drilled into the jump standards. Inevitably, no matter how careful you are, there may be some splintering of wood. The dremel can get into the tiny areas where the sander can't go. By paying attention to the small details, you will create amazing jumps that will rival the professionals.

5. Towels

I know what you're thinking…towels? Really? Yes, towels. Hand towels are great for wiping away the dusty residue that gets on your wood. It is a good idea to wipe down the wood one last time before painting.

6. Leaf Blower

This is great for blowing the sawdust off your jumps after sanding and to keep your area clean after cutting the wood.

7. Paint Brushes, Rollers, and Paint Pans.

Self-explanatory, but an important tool nonetheless. The better quality brushes you buy, the longer they will last. Take care of your brushes and the will last forever. I personally like Purdy brushes. They are expensive, but the paint job is great.

8. Measuring Tape

An indispensable item you will need over and over for all of your jump building. I actually have two in my immediate work area because I always seem to lose one when I need it.

9. Sharpie Marker

I love my sharpie for marking on my wood where I will be cutting it. Yes, it is permanent, but the thick black line it creates make it easy to see the line I am going to be cutting. When I sand down the wood pieces, the ink gets sanded of. If you like you can use a pencil, but my first choice is always a sharpie.

This list is by no means all encompassing. Add to it or change it to fit your needs. These are the tools I use and find that I need when making my jumps. I also have over run our garage, and turned it into my workshop, it isn't fancy but it works. You won't need a lot of space, but you will need enough room to fit an eight foot piece of wood that you can maneuver around. When the wood is cut up and not put together, it doesn't take much space. However, once you start building the standards, and painting the rails, that does take a fair amount of room. Doing one or two at a time is the easiest. It's when you start building a complete course of eight to ten jumps that the space tends to be taken up!

10. Wood

Yes, wood is a tool. Not only will you be using it for your jumps, but the left over pieces come in handy as well. If you take several two foot long sections of a 4x4, they help to raise wood up from the floor giving you a sturdy pace to cut. I try not to throw out the larger pieces of scraps, as they could be useful for some other project, or could become a useful tool for making future jumps.

And lastly, and most importantly make sure you have protective eyewear, and gloves. If there is an opportunity to have wood fly into your eyes, it will. Also if you have long hair, tie it back, and make sure it can't fall forward into your work area.

This list is by no means complete, but these are the basics you will need to get started with your jump building. At the end of the book you will find a complete shopping list if everything I use when building my jumps, and hopefully it will be helpful for you when you are building your jumps.

Ok, you have your tools, your workspace is ready, and you know how to be safe while working with power tools, so let's build some jumps!

Chapter 3

Building A Basic Jump Standard

This is the best of the best, a basic jump standard. For this example I am building a four-foot jump standard. However, you can make it any size you like. Starting with a four foot standard keeps things simple, because you have a basic 4x4x8' and you are cutting it in half, which makes your two jump standards with one cut.

Shopping List:

(1) 4x4"x8' that has been cut into two 48" sections

(2) 2x6"x8' that has been cut into 16" sections

(16) 2.5" decking screws (the ones with an included drill bit work the best)

This is the only wood you will need, a 4x4x8 and two 2x6x8's. I'm not kidding, see…I told you this would be easy!

Mark and measure where you will be cutting your wood…

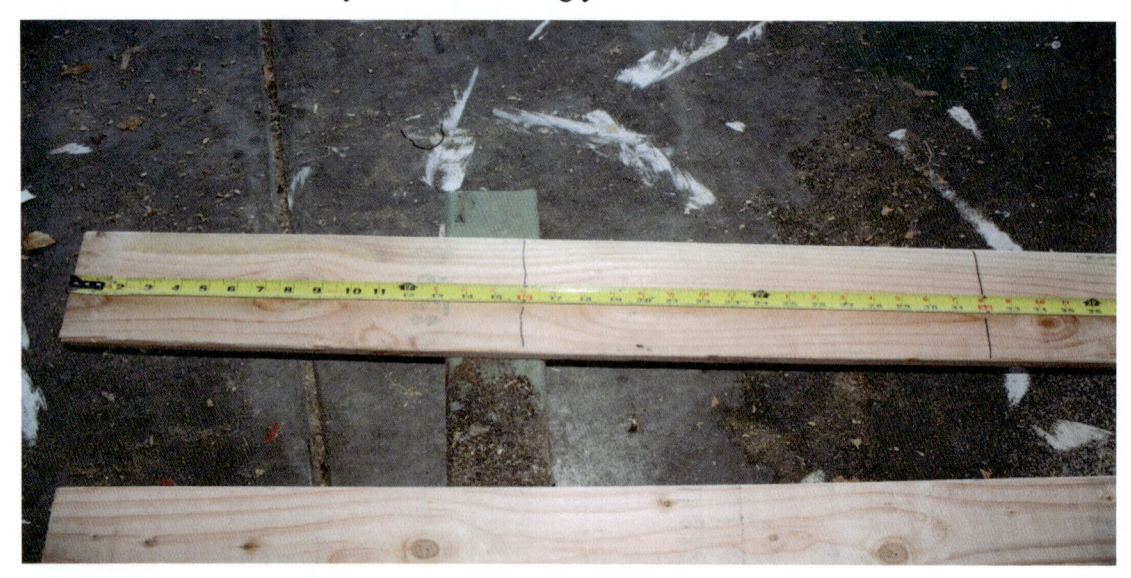

And your finished wood will look like this:

Now, with all your pieces cut, take the 4' long pieces of your 4x4, and you are going to mark where you want your holes to be for your jump cups. Trust me, it is a lot easier to do this part before you put the feet on your jump standard.

When making your marks of where you are going to be drilling, in order to keep it centered measure 1.5 inches from one side, and place a dot. Do the same thing on the other side, 1.5 inches. You will then have a channel down the center where you can drill your holes, and have them centered on the standard. The best way I have found to do this is with a jump cup, and color a dot where the hole line up. For my jumps, I space my holes starting at 12", and then every 6". My highest jumping height with these four-foot standards is 3'6". For myself, this is a realistic jumping height, so I don't need to have five foot standards, but that doesn't mean you need to stop where I did! Also cutting holes in the wood is MUCH easier to use a spade bit in your drill than a drill bit. The biggest difference is the spade bit doesn't splinter the wood like a drill bit will.

I have heard there are tricks you can do to make it so the wood doesn't splinter, but I don't know what they are, so this works the best for me. The spade bit seems faster than the drill bit, as well as it is easier to drill straight with this type of bit instead of a standard drill bit. You can easily see the holes that this spade bit created, and look, no splintered wood! And the back looks the same. This spade bit is ½ " which works perfect for regular size jump cups.

A word of advice when drilling these holes, use the jump cups you will be using for marking your holes! Not all jump cups are the same, and if you have a different type cup you will be using vs. what you used to drill your holes, you will be very frustrated when the cup won't work on your jump standard. And yes, I give this advice because it happened to me.

After you have completed all of your drilled holes, sand all of the wood pieces down. I didn't put a picture of that, because sanding is simple. You just turn on the sander, go with the grain of the wood until everything is smooth. Make sure to take all of the edges are smooth.

You may notice in the next picture, my 2x6 x 16" look a little different. Can you see the difference? I cut the top corner off, making it more of a rounded appearance, making it safer if someone were to fall and hit their head on the corner. It would still hurt, but with the corners rounded down, there is less of a risk of an injury.

I feel this is a very important part of "finishing" the standard. It makes it appear professional, and it is safe. I know that having the dimensions might help some, but there is nothing to this. Take your sharpie, and draw a line on the corner. It takes off the sharp corner, and with a little sanding, you have a very safe and atheistically pleasing footer for your standard.

You don't have to do it, but it only takes about five minutes to do enough of the footings for three sets of standards, so I do it. And I am still trying to find a use for the little triangle pieces it creates!

The next step is attaching the footers. I am no carpenter, so I am all about the easy way. I line up the footer so it is flush with the base of the standard. This picture isn't a good example of the footer lined up, but I was trying to show you 'easy' as far as placing the screw.

You line up the footer, and by predrilling the screw, you can hold the footer in place better because you aren't trying to hold to wobbly pieces of wood while trying to force a screw through the both of them. I like using Douglas fir wood for the footers. You can use whatever type of wood you like, but the Douglas fir wood seems 'soft', making it easy for the screws to go in.

Once you have the screw in place, you are going to flip the base, and do it again. Don't be tempted to put two screws in at this point. By only having one screw in place, the footer will have a little 'play' to it so when you stand it up you can make sure it is square. It is a lot easier to screw the footer on in this manner, trust me…again, learned from experience. Just line up the corner of the footer, and then make sure the bottom of the base of your jump standard matches the bottom of the footer. If you like, you can use a level or a square to make sure you have it right.

It's hard to see, but there is just one screw in place. I sink it down deep, so there isn't the possibility it could work out. If it could, it could create a sharp edge, which could cause a safety concern. By sinking the screw a little deep into the wood, I am giving myself an area I will caulk later on.

You just keep flipping, and driving in one screw on each flip. In this picture, you can see there is a little play, which will allow me to square up the entire piece when it is standing.

Now stand the jump up, you will have three of the footers secured, and placing the last one has to be done when the jump is standing. However, you have three pieces of wood now to give stability. So all you have to do now is secure the last footer.

So the last footer is in place, and now I press all the footers down to make sure they are all level. This is another good time to use a level to make sure everything is level and square.

After you have done that, you are going to drill a screw so that it crosses the footer, and goes into the other footer. Spin the jump around to each footer, and repeat the process. So when you are completed, each footer will have two screws, one in the base of your jump standard, and one connecting the footers to each other. When I am creating larger jump standards, like five and six foot tall, I will add one more screw for extra precaution on each footer. I want these things solid, and it only takes a few minutes to add four more screws.

Once all of the footers have been secured to the base of your jump standard, you may notice there are some gaps, as you can see in the picture above, but that isn't a big deal, it will be sealed with caulking in our next phase.

And below, you will see the finished product, as far as the construction is concerned. This is a good time to go over everything one more time with a sander, and then blow everything off with a leaf blower, blow dryer or shop vac. Anything will work, and it's an important step not to overlook. By sanding one last time, you might find a couple little rough spots you missed. Everything you can do to make it perfect will make your jump standards stand out from your competition, if you are building these to sell. Or if you are building them for yourself, they will be that much more enjoyable because you not only built these yourself, you did an outstanding job.

And that is pretty much it. If you wanted to, you could use this as it is. However, if you used Douglas fir lumber, like I did, you aren't quite finished. If I were to put these out in my riding area right now, they wouldn't last very long. Partially from the weather, and partially from my two horses who were apparently beavers in their past lives. So in order to protect my jumps from the elements, and my animals, I finish my jump standards completely.

Caulking is the next step. I use regular latex painters caulk in white. Another tip of advice, make sure the caulk you will be using is paintable. Silicone caulk does not work very well, and is almost impossible to get paint to stick to it. It will eventually cover the silicone, but it isn't worth the brain damage it causes trying to get the caulk covered.

Cutting the tip of the caulk at an angle, and only about an inch down keeps the caulking under my control. Again, learning how to master the caulking gun and where to cut the tube of caulk is one of those 'things' I have learned by trial and error. There is no right or wrong way to caulk, but it can be messy, so having a roll of paper towels close by is helpful.

With the majority of the work done, now it is time to paint the standards. This is where the fun comes in! These are your jumps, you can paint them however you like.

When painting, it works best to do it in several phases. First, make sure the standards are free from dust, and the caulk is dry. Paint one coat of your color choice. I typically will use a roller, and cover each of the four sides, turning it away from me, which makes it so I can paint each foot of the base as well.

A word of caution when painting your bases, if you do not want your area to end up looking like a giant piece of abstract art, cover the floor, otherwise you will end up with multiple patterns of different colors of paint all over the area you are painting.

Notice the floor of my garage? All of those random white and green spots are where the bases of jumps I have painted were. For me, I don't really care, but if you want to keep your garage floor looking pristine, I would recommend putting down newspaper, or a giant tarp to protect the floor.

Here is the finished product…

This was an afternoon of building, and another several afternoons of caulking, painting and finishing. The rail in the foreground is an example of how you can paint your rails. I didn't tape off the colors, so the edges aren't crisp, but if you don't have tape you can see that you can still make rails that will be fun to go over once you have the finished product.

Also, when painting poles, you want to have them up off the ground, and you can use whatever you have. Notice what I used? Kitty litter buckets! These work great for painting rails.

And don't think you have to stick with a solid color for your jump standards. Use your imagination to create a work of art!

Chapter 4

Building A Wing Standard

It may seem like a daunting task, but it isn't that bad. In fact, building a pair of wing standards is relatively simple if you have already built a couple of stick standards. The principles are the same, however there are a few added steps.

First, you will need 1 entire landscaping timber for each standard, so to make a pair of wing standards that are four foot tall, you will need 2 landscaping timbers. So it does cost more to make a pair of wing standards, however as you can see in the picture above the extra cost is worth it when you can create something like this.

To create a pair of four-foot wing standards you will need:

(2) landscaping timbers, eight foot long

(1) 2 x 4 x 8' Douglas fir lumber

(1) 2 x 6 x 8' Douglas fir lumber

(8) 1 x 3 x 6' fence pickets

3" decking screws

1 5/8" decking screws

To begin, take your landscaping timbers and measure them off in four foot sections. You will be cutting the timbers in half.

You will do this to two landscaping timbers, so you will have four equal pieces, each four feet in length.

Then, you will match up the pieces so they are equal on their height and width apart from each other. I find the easiest way to do this is to use one of your fence pickets, or an extra piece of wood at the base (bottom) of your wing standard.

In this picture, I am only showing you lining up the bottom so it is equal, because as you can see, this wing has uneven ends. In this example, I have a five-foot end that will tie into a three foot end piece. However, regardless of how the jump will be, equal or at an angle, the base must remain level.

After you get the base squared up, measure how wide you want the wing to be. I like about eighteen inches. And you are going to cut your 2 x 4 x 8 into four equal sized pieces (18 inches).

Then you are going to put it in the open area between your two end pieces. Secure each corner to the ends pieces of the landscaping timbers.

This isn't the best picture, but you can see where you are going to secure the pieces of 2 x 4 to the ends of your wing.

Measure off from the top and bottom, making sure you keep the 2 x 4 sections even on both ends of your wing. Then you are going to screw each corner of the 2 x 4 with a three inch screw securing it to the ends of your wing. You will have to screw at a 45 degree angle in order to have the screw go through the 2 x 4 and end up in the landscaping timber, or wing end.

Make sure you are putting pressure on both the 2 x 4 and the landscaping timber to keep the ends flush and together. Also, do this slowly in order to keep the 2 x 4 even, and where you want it to be permanently.

Once you have completed securing all of the 2 x 4's, your 'frame will look like an H. Once this is done, you can remove your end piece, because your frame will be done, and you will be attaching your pickets to the 2 x 4 section of your frame, or the middle of your wing standard.

Now, put the uncut fence pickets on the 2 x 4. Make sure the tops are all level, and measure off how high you want them to be from the bottom. A word of advice, keep them at least nine inches from the bottom, because you will need to have a little room from where your feet will be placed. Once you have the general idea of where you want your pickets, spacing, length, etc. Measure off where you will be cutting the bottom of each one using your measuring tape and sharpie to create your line. Cut all of your pickets, and then lay them out again over the 2 x 4 section of each wing standard. I say each one, because it is best to create two standards at one time, this way you can make sure they are equal in height and size. And it is best to create a pair of standards at the same time to make sure they match.

Once you are happy with how your pickets measure up, you can attach each one to the 2 x 4. Use one screw on the top 2 x 4 section, and one on the bottom using your 1 5/8" decking screw. After all of your pickets are secure, you are now ready to attach the feet to your wing standard.

Take your 2 x 6 x 8 and cut off four pieces of 16". These will be your feet. Cut the top corners off (it will be a little triangle) So you will be cutting off the two top corners of the 2 x 8 x 16". Sand down each piece before attaching it to your wing standard for a finished look. Trust me, do the sanding before you attach the foot, it is much easier to sand a small piece of wood instead of sanding a four foot tall awkward piece of wood!

After you have cut and sanded the feet, attach them to the frame of your wing standard, like this:

You will attach a foot to the outside of your landscaping timber. I like to square up where the feet will go, so there is approximately six inches in front of the timber, and six inches behind. It also makes it easier if you start two screws, and then drive them through the landscaping timber. After I have attached each foot, I go back and add one more screw for a little bit of added attachment.

Depending on what color you are going to be painting your wings, you can wait and attach your pickets after you have painted the main frame of the wing standard. It is an extra step, but it does make it easier if you are going to be painting the pickets a different color than the frame. And even if you are going to be painting the entire wing standard the same, it is easier of the picket is already painted because there are less little nooks and crannies you have to get your paint brush into.

After the jump is fully assembled, this is when I measure off where the holes are going to be for the jumps cups. The jump is very sturdy and stable at this point, so you can lay it flat and measure your holes, and then drill away!

This is what your finished wing standards will look like! You can see there is a little spacing where the 2 x 4's butt up against the landscaping timber. This is easily finished off with a bead of caulk on each area of where your 2 x 4 meets up with the landscaping timber.

This is another example of what you can create by getting a little creative.

Chapter 5

Paint

Choosing the right paint will make a big difference in the quality of your jumps. Paint not only makes your jumps look good, but it also helps provide extra durability to all of your hard work. By painting your jumps, you are creating a barrier between the wood and the weather. This will not only beautify your jumps, but it will make them last a lot longer than they would if you chose not to paint them.

There are different sheens of paint, and different classifications of paint. All of my jumps are painted with thick exterior semi-gloss paint. It gives a slight sheen to the jump element, and it seems to last really well.

The sheen seems to be a personal preference, and I haven't found one sheen that lasts longer than the other. But the most important element of the paint is it has to be exterior paint. Don't get frugal on this part, unless you have an indoor arena that will house your jumps at all times, and even then, you could have a paint failure due to the elements.

Exterior paint has been specially formulated to withstand being outside, all the time. If you put interior pain on your jumps, they won't last. At first they will be fine. But after a year or two, you will notice the paint is bubbling, or flaking off. This is because interior paint is not meant to be used outside. And if you decide to just cover up the paint, it will continue to deteriorate. The only solution is to sand it all off, and start over with exterior paint.

The easiest paint I have found to work with is latex. The clean-up is simple, just soap and water, and it dries relatively quickly. Enamels and oil based paints are messier, and you have to clean your brushes with mineral spirits. For me, cleaning my brushed with a flammable substance isn't a good idea, so I stick with the latex paints. You can find latex enamels, such as Krylon and they clean up with soap and water too.

You will find a lot of the painting you will be doing is white. White goes with everything, and works great to make your rails stand out for visibility concerns. But all white paints are not created equally. Don't be tempted to buy the cheapest white paint you can find. It will take many more coats of paint of the cheap paint to equal two coats of the higher quality white paint. You will spend more in time and money with the cheaper paint, so do it right the first time and get the better quality white paint.

And even though your initial investment will be more, it makes sense to buy your white paint in the five gallon buckets. You will use a lot of it, so by purchasing it in the larger size, you will really be saving yourself money. And if you can wait until spring, around Memorial Day, or the Fall, around Labor Day, the big home improvement stores usually have the paint on sale. This is when I try to bulk up on my five gallon purchases.

When applying your paint, make sure you allow time for each layer to dry completely. This will help with using less paint per jumping element. And if you keeping applying heavy coats of paint, you can end up with runs, or cracks, or bubbling. SO take the extra time and do it right the first time. You will save yourself time and money in the long run!

If you haven't noticed it yet, I tend to be a little bit of a cheapskate when it comes to buying supplies for jump building. And I am the same way with my paint. Typically I will complete several jump sets and end up with a quarter of a gallon of paint left. I don't throw it out though, that would be wasteful. No, I keep my left overs of paint, and when I want a new color, or need to make a lighter color, I blend the colors together.

I remember one time I was making a small set of jumps for a lady, and she requested a set of brown jumps. This was fine, but I didn't have any brown paint, nor any money to go buy a gallon of brown paint. But I did have some dark green paint, and I had a lot of red, and a small amount of a dark brownish black. So I took the three containers of left over paint, and came up with a really nice chocolate brown!

By saving the paints I had used before, I was able to make a completely new color, and didn't have to go out to buy more paint.

Did you know that by mixing green and red paint, you will get brown? Or if you mix blue and red, you will get purple? And of course, mixing yellow and blue will give you green. But, if you have a dark hunter green, and add some yellow to it, you will get a really nice Kermit the Frog green!

And by taking left over colors and adding white you will get a really nice complementary color of your original color. For instance, the blue jump below. I had the original blue paint, and wanted a lighter blue for the accent color. I simply added some white paint, and got a very nice complimentary blue for the jump without having to match colors, or spend extra money.

So be cheap and creative in your paint selections, and you will be able to come up with many different possibilities!

Chapter 6

Rails and Poles

Creating rails and poles for your jumps is relatively easy. Again, you are only limited by your imagination! When I am making rails, I want them to be sturdy and inexpensive. This can create a challenge.

You can use PVC pipe, but this can be more expensive per rail than using wood. The benefit to using PVC pipe is that it is readily available in ten and twelve-foot lengths, which isn't always the case with wood. If you are choosing to use PVC, you can add sand to the poles, and put end pieces in each end, which will keep your sand inside, and add weight to the poles. The total cost of each rail with paint, end caps, and sand is about twenty dollars.

The problem with using PVC for rails is horses don't learn to respect them. They are lightweight and flimsy. Many times horses will learn to be lazy when jumping PVC rails because there is not enough substance to them. They can drop their legs, and if they hit the rail, it will just tap them. However, if they hit something that has a little more 'ouch' to it, they learn to really tuck their front legs because they don't want to hit that, it hurts!

But finding wood poles that you can use for jump rails can be very expensive. You can find unpainted 3.5" poles for about twenty-five dollars apiece through jump companies, before shipping. Or you can buy 4 x 4 x 10's and cut the sides at a 45 degree angle and create octagon type rails which work great, but again are expensive, and labor intensive.

A very good alternative that is a lot cheaper is the cherry tone landscaping timbers that are at most home improvement super stores. I don't think I need to tell you where. You can buy one landscaping timber for three dollars most times of the year, and close to Memorial Day, I have seen them as low as one dollar, per piece. That is a huge savings over PVC, and 4 x 4's and they are sturdy.

The only drawback that some may think is the length. Typically these 3" x 3" landscaping timbers come in eight-foot lengths only. To some, this may be a deal breaker, but think about it, you are working your horse at home over jumps with less width. Your horse gets used to jumping 'smaller' jumps at home. And when you get to the horse show, the jumps are wider, ten to twelve feet. Jumping the longer jumps will seem easier, because you have been working over 'smaller' jumps at home. And just because the overall length is less, you can add more poles, and more fillers, creating very similar horse show jumps at your own home. Your horse will be more willing to jump at the shows, because you have created similar jumping elements at home. So my choice is for the eight foot long cherry tone landscaping timbers for three dollars every time.

The biggest tip I can give to you when painting your rails is the tape. You can use regular masking tape, but you will not get super crisp lines. You can use the blue painters tape, but again, the paint tends to bleed through, and you don't get the crisp lines. In the picture below, I used the blue painter's tape when creating my lines for the rails. Even though I was careful, you can see where the paint was still able to bleed through, creating a fuzzy edge to the difference in paint colors. This isn't a big deal really, unless you want perfect, crisp, and definite definition between your colors.

In the next two examples, I switched to the green frog tape, and the results show.

See the difference? The lines are crisp, and edges are perfect. Even though my rails are not perfectly round, the crispness of the definition in the pain shows, and when you are creating jumps for others, it's the little details that count, and will see your products.

Even when you have contrasting colors, which will take multiple layers of paint, there is no bleed through with the frog tape.

The best part about making your own rails is there no right or wrong way. If you can imagine it, you can make it happen. When you are picturing the striping of your rails, measure off the specs on your rail. I will typically measure and step back to make sure it looks good. Keep the stripes the same size, and equal. And what I mean by that is easiest explained by looking at the above picture.

Before you begin painting, sand the rail down, and remove any labels. Sometime the rails will have splits, which can be easily filled with either paintable caulk (my first choice) or spackle. After the caulking has dried, you can begin to paint. I will paint the entire rail the solid, or background color. Another tip, if the rail is going to be white with colored stripes, my first two coats are usually primer coats first. When those have dried, I will do my finishing coat of white semi-gloss exterior paint.

What I did was measure the middle of the rail, which is four feet. I put a little mark at four feet, and then I measure one foot on either side of that mark, going from three feet to five feet. This gives me my stripe in the middle, and it is centered on the rail. Hopefully, that makes sense.

Then, I went to each end, and measures one foot in, and put a little mark with my sharpie, measure off an additional six inches, and put another mark. After everything is marked, I apply the frog tape around the area I want to apply the second, or third color, depending on how many colors I am applying.

And that's it! The easiest way to get the stripes painted is to set up your jump standards in your work area. This way you can easily turn the rails and make sure you have completely covered the area you are working on.

First, let me apologize for the mess. Yes, this is actually my messy garage, and it doubles as my work area for my jump building. However, aside from the mess, you can see my standards, with the jump cups and the rails I was working on. If you look closely, you can see the fuzzy edges of the yellow. This is the frog tape, protecting the edges of my purple.

Play with your striping. Check out Google images for ideas, and paint some stripes!

Chapter 7

Gates

Even though gates are more expensive to make than the rails, it does make sense to have at least one in your ring of jumps. The biggest benefit to gates that I have found is they create great filler for a jump. They fill the empty space, making the jump seem more solid for the horse.

When I make a gate, I use two 2x4x8's and depending on how you want the pickets to be spaced, regular fence pickets work great. They are very inexpensive, and you can typically get at least four small pickets for your gate from each full size picket.

I lay out both 2x4's so they are equal, and on the 2x4 that will be the bottom of my gate, I cut 6-8" off. This will give you some clearance, and by using an even number that you have cut off, you will divide that (6 inches will equal a 3' mark on wither end of your remaining full size 2x4. For the rest of this example, we will say we kept it at the 6 inch mark.)

After that, I cut my pickets. Depending on how tall you want your gate will determine how tall you will make your pickets. I usually will cut mine about 12 to 15 inches.

Now is where the creative part come in…

Lay out your 2x4's again, but measure off 3" on the full size 2x4. This is where you will place your first picket/ It should have a 3" edge on the top board, and it should be on the end of the bottom board. Make sure your pickets are lined up, and secure each side down with a screw at the top of your picket, and one at the bottom. For the screws, I like to use 1 5/8" decking screws. They don't come out on the front of the gate, and the circumference is a little bit smaller, so they do not seem to split the pickets when they are secured down.

With the two ends of the gate secured, now you can play around and configure the rest of your pickets how you would like them to go. Here are some examples:

This is a simple straight gate. Each of the spaces in between the pickets have been measured off to have equal spaces.

This gate is just a modified version of the simple gate. The ends are just tilted at an angle. I first measured the center, and secured the two center pickets, and then worked my way out, keeping the same amount of pickets on either side.

In both of these examples, all of the wood is secured completing the gate, and then each side was painted several times, allowing for each coat to try before putting on the next.

This is yet another version. The main difference is the pickets were all painted prior to assembling the gate. The last two pickets, and the frame of the gate were painted and completed prior to placing the white pickets.

This is a solid color gate, finding the center first, I then cut two pickets equal length for the ends. Then two longer pieces were cut for the angled pieces and attached to the back. Everything was then painted.

The last example is a solid appearing gate. This is great for making a jump appear 'solid' for your horse. And if you get good pickets, they will line up pretty well, but if not, a line of caulk down the back seam will join everything together.

These of course are not all of the possibilities, but it gives you a good starting point. Gates can be tall, or short. They can be solid colors, or different colors. Whatever works for you, can be done and still create a beautiful and easy piece to build to your jump course. They are also great for changing things up. But as I stated in the beginning of this chapter, they are more expensive to build than just plain poles. However, once you see a jump built using several poles and a gate with a flower box, you will be very happy you did it!

Chapter 8

Planks

Making planks is simple, and depending on your creativity, you can create some pretty cool fillers for your jumps. Planks can be made from either 2 x 6's, 2 x 8's, or even 2 x 10's. You can keep it simple, and paint the planks solid colors, or you can paint a pattern on each one, or stones, or bricks. Really, anything you can think of you can add to the plank element of your jumps.

There is minimal cutting that need to be done with a plank. I find the wider the plank, the larger area you will have to place in the jump cup. Start with the piece of wood up on a platform. Then you will take your measuring tape, and measure in how far you want to have your 'plank' end sit in the jump cup. Usually, I have mine go in four to six inches.

Mark with a sharpie where your in point will be, like I said I put mine usually at the six inch point. Then, measure how thick your plank end will be. Depending on the length of the board will determine how thick the plank end will be for me when I am creating a plank. I like it to be relatively thick, in case it bounces out of the jump cup when it is being used. I don't want the end to break off, and the thicker the plank end means it is less likely to break off. I have seen these planks dropped, and with the thick ends, they are not in danger of breaking. However, if you were to have a thin plank end, say two inches thick, by six inches in length, if it bounces it might break off the end. These are just some tips to keep in mind when you are determining how you want your plank ends to look.

Here are some examples:

These planks are 2 x 8 x 8. You can see where it goes about 6 inches in length, and the height of the end is about five inches, so I cut out three inches from the bottom. So when you cut it out, you will end up with a little rectangle of wood. These little rectangles are great to have as 'feet' when you are making flower boxes, so don't throw them away!

As you can see from the above picture, my cuts overlapped a little. This happened because I used my circular saw when making the cuts. And you will find, when using the circular saw, when you flip the plank over, your cuts will not match up. This can be avoided by using a jig saw into the corner, or you could fill in the little cut through mark with caulking or spackle. It is up to you, and if you want perfection.

Here is another example of the plank ends:

This is a longer plank, 2 x 10 x 8. That allowed me to make a thicker end of the plank that will sit in the jump cup.

The finished product can be a nice extra element to add to your ring of jumps.

These are just some very basic examples of planks that you can create easily. You can add other elements, or even paint each side differently allowing more flexibility of your jumps.

Chapter 9

Flowerboxes

The last items to build for your jump course are probably the simplest to construct. And, depending on the size of jump standard you constructed, you might have extra pieces lying around. Even though the flower boxes might be the easiest for you to build, they are no less important than any other piece of your jump set.

Flower boxes create a simple, changeable filler that can be placed in many different areas of your jumps. They complete the entire jump, and they offer color and pop to your jumps. They are easily switched up, keeping things fresh for the horses, and always adding new elements to your jumping routine.

So even though they are simple, they are a very important aspect of each horse jump you will be using them with.

Depending on the size of rails you are using, you will be able to change the size of flower boxes you will be making. The flower box above is one from a pair of four-foot long flower boxes. It is made from a 4x4 post. Yes, the same ones you made your jump standards from. The holes on the top are drilled with the 1/2" spade bit. But the holes do not go all the way through. If you place the bit up to the side of the 4x4, and adjust it to the point where it almost goes through, but not quite, and take a piece of your tape, and wind it around the shaft of the bit, marking the level of how deep you will be drilling your holes. This is an easy step that will prevent you from drilling all the way through your flower box.

Measure off the holes, and determine how you would like your spacing to be. Mark where you would like the holes to be with your sharpie. Once you have your holes measured, you are going to flip over the section, and you are going to attach your feet.

Using a left over piece either from a 2 x 4, or 2 x 6, measure off 6", and cut two identical pieces. Then, attach them to the bottom of your flower box. For whatever reason, I have better luck with the 2x4's not splitting, so I tend to use 2x4 scraps for the feet of my flower boxes. The spacing from either end is up to you, I personally move my feet in about 4" from either end.

Once you have your feet securely attached, flip the flower box over and drill your holes. Remember, only go down as far as your tape allows, when the tape hits the edge of the hole you are drilling, stop. You don't want to go all the way through on these holes, as you did for your jump standard holes.

The amount of holes you create is up to you. Depending on if you want to add a lot of flowers, or just a few. Keep this in mind when you are planning your holes for drilling. After you have drilled everything, sand it all smooth and remove any remaining dust. Then, pick your paint, allow to dry and you have a pair of flower boxes. Simple, but necessary, and they really do complete the jump.

For your flowers, you can purchase premade sets of flowers made specifically for horse jumps. But if you have learned anything about me, you know I will be making these myself as well. A set of flowers retail for anywhere between twenty and forty dollars, depending on what you want. However, you can purchase silk flowers at discount stores, or craft stores when they are on sale for usually one-tenth the cost as the ready-made sets. You will also have the added benefit of coordinating the colors to what you want them to be.

I think the best set of flowers I made actually came from three full bunches of mixed 'springtime' flowers I purchased about ten years ago at a craft store. (Ok, it was Hobby Lobby!) I remember buying them on sale, using them in my house decorating for about three or four years, and then I stuck them away in a box. Since they had outlived their usefulness in the house, I felt better about repurposing them for my horse jumps. My kind of recycling! The flowers in the first picture of this chapter were the flowers I used.

All you have to do, is section off three 'stems', cut them with wire cutters, and bunch them together. Then, using duct tape, I secure the little group of flowers together. Do this as many times as you need for your flower boxes. I don't leave my flowers out in the boxes however. I worry that my curious horses might think they are a treat, so they are put into a plastic tub, and brought out when I am going to be using them to jump. This has made my flowers last a very long time, saving them from the elements, and my horses.

This is a set of flowers I made for a pair of three-foot flower boxes. You can see the zebra duct tape on the bottom, holding the little bunches together.

When you are making your flower boxes, you don't have to use the 4x4's. The cherry landscaping timbers (remember, three dollars a pole….a great deal) work great. Another option I have done is using 2x6 and a 1x4. The 2x6 is for the height, and the 1x4 is the top where you will be drilling your holes. By having it 6" high, you can drill your flower holes all the way through. You could put a bottom on it if you wanted to, but I just use the 2x6, making it easier to move around. The photo below is an example of one of the 2x6 flower boxes I have made.

I kept the holes pretty close on this one, so the flowers would add fullness to the bottom of the jump I created this for.

And again, get creative! You don't have to have the typical flower box just under the first rail of your jump. Add some accent flower boxes to make your jumps stand out, and seem more substantial. Depending on how tall you have been making your jump standards, you will undoubtedly have some extra pieces of wood. Use them! See what you can come up with!

And how about adding some flower boxes to your wing standards? Not only is it pretty, but it adds some extra stability to your wings. You can paint them all the same color, like I did in this example, or change it up and make it an added art element to your standards!

A simple addition for stability and it's functional too.

Chapter 10

Building A Simple Jump, The Shopping List

This is what I consider a simple jump. It consists of a pair of four-foot standards, two rails, two small flower boxes, and two pair of jump cups. Everything you will need to create this jumps are as follows:

(4) Cherry Tone Landscaping Timbers ($3.00 apiece, $12.00 total)

(1) 2 x 4 x 10 ($3.50 apiece, $7.00 total)

(28) 3" Decking Screws (1-pound box for $9.50)

(1) Tube of Painter's Caulk ($1.25)

White Exterior Semi-Gloss Paint ($19.95 for a gallon)

Dark Blue Exterior Semi-Gloss Paint ($19.95 for a gallon)

Frog Tape ($5.37)

(2) Pair of Jump Cups (Jeffer's is the cheapest, 4.99 for a pair of plastic cups, $10.00 total)

Miscellaneous Flowers for the Flower Boxes ($5.00)

Total cost to make a simple jump: $90.00

I know what you're thinking. "But you told me earlier I can make a jump for less than $25.00? Why is it $90.00 now? And the reason is this, you can't buy 28 screws, or 1 ounce of paint. So yes, the initial investment is more, but when you average out your cost, you can make a simple jump for $25.00 when you average in the cost of your screws, paint and necessary supplies to create your jump.

Keep in mind this list does not include your tools that you will need, but after you have read the first few chapters in this book, you will know what tools you need. The total cost for your shopping list may vary from what I actually paid, so shop around to get the best deal so you can create your jump for less money. Also, the cost of certain materials may be more expensive, like the screws, but with a single 1 pound box of screws you can build at least 10 pairs of schooling standards.

Get creative and try different color combinations. You have the materials, so make some jumps. Ideas of color combinations include your barn colors, your favorite sports team colors, or even keeping the colors the same as your home. The possibilities are endless!

Every one of these jumps is derived from the simple jump principle.

Chapter 11

Building An Oxer Jump, The Shopping list

To build a jump, it helps to know what the names are. And an oxer, is a jump that has two elements too it which will create more width when the horse jumps. As the previous chapter created a shopping list for a simple vertical jump, you can take it one step further and create two vertical, or simple jumps to make one jumping obstacle, which would be an oxer. You can further it by creating three parts to one jump, so it could be an oxer, and a combination jump, meaning there are multiple jumps within a relatively short span of space, making it a combination jump.

So let's keep it simple, and create an oxer from two of the simple vertical jumps. In this example, we will be creating an Aspen tree oxer.

To create this jump, this will be our shopping list:

(4) Cherry tone Landscaping Timbers ($12.00)

(2) 2 x 4 x 10 Douglas Fir Lumber ($7.00)

(2) Pairs of Jump Cups ($10.00)

Black Exterior Semi-Gloss Paint ($19.95)

(32) 3" Decking Screws ($0.00)

(1) Tube Painter's Caulk ($0.00)

White Exterior Semi-Gloss Paint ($0.00)

Total Cost to create an Aspen tree oxer jump: $48.95

See? You have already purchased your screws, painter's caulk and paint. So your cost in creating this oxer is less than the first jump you created!

The examples provided are just to show you that you can create quality horse jumps for yourself, or to sell for not very much money. It will take some time, but with practice you can create beautiful jumps that you will be proud to own!

Chapter 12

Resources

While I was creating this book, I found the internet to be a very valuable resource for not only getting ideas of different jumps to create, but also for comparing prices of items I would be needing to build my jumps as well as looking at professional jump companies to determine the cost of building jumps. Below is a list of different sites I found helpful when building my jumps.

Jeffers Equine

http://www.jefferspet.com/jeffers-equine/camid/EQU/ca/134/

This site has the best price on plastic jump cups if you are purchasing them singularly, and they are fast at shipping.

Country Supply

http://www.horse.com/

This site has metal jump cups at the best price I have found, and if you order multiple sets, you get an even bigger discount! They are also State Line Tack, so both sites have the same prices, and a large selection.

Dover's Saddlery

http://www.doversaddlery.com/

Dover's has jump cups, and they have a selection of jumps you can see on their website. These are great to look at and get ideas when you are creating your own jumps. Plus, you can see how expensive jumps are if you were to purchase them from a supplier. For me, this was a major motivator when deciding to make my own jumps.

Google

http://www.google.com

Google is the best search engine I have found. Not only can you find different website for what you are searching for, you can also change from search to images. I find this helpful when I am looking for different ideas when making jumps.

Home Depot

http://www.homedepot.com

Home Depot is a great place to buy paint, and the materials needed for building your jumps. They have the added benefit of allowing you to place your order online, and they will text you when it is ready to pick up. This is very helpful to me, because they pull all the wood I need, and have it all ready to go at the front of the store. I just stop in at the customer service desk and they go get my order. Plus, the help me load the wood. This is a huge time saver, and when I am making a couple set of jumps, any time I can save is a bonus. Also when I go to any home improvement store I always stop by their 'oops' pain section and will usually find a gallon of paint I can use. And when I can buy a gallon of paint for seven dollars vs. twenty dollars, the savings makes it so worth it!

This is a list of places that I use regularly when building jumps for myself, or for others. It is by no means all inclusive, and I am sure you have places you can find close to you with just as good of deals. But these places have always worked out very well for me, well enough to stand out in my memory and want me to share it with you.

I hope you have found this book useful, and I hope you are able to realize you don't have to spend a lot of money to make some jumps for yourself. I wish you luck in building your own jumps, and I hope you are very proud of yourself when you have them done! Good luck and congratulations on taking the first step to building your own jumps!

About The Author

Lisa Goodwin

    I am a complete horse lover. I was bitten by the horse bug over forty years ago. There isn't a memory I have that does not include horses in one way or another. Every aspect of my life has always involved horses. But not being made of money, I have always had to be thrifty when it comes to my passion of horses.

    As an avid competitor and horse enthusiast, I am always looking for ways to make showing and riding affordable for myself and others. About two years ago I decided to make horse jumps after I saw how expensive they are. And when it got too cold to make jumps, I needed something else to do to keep me busy, so I decided to write a book with the hopes of helping others be able to make their own jumps.

    I still sell jumps, and because of the cost of shipping, it tends to be to people in Colorado mostly, but occasionally I will have someone order some jumps from a neighboring state. I love seeing the expression on their face when they see the jumps I have made for them. There is no better feeling! So if you would like to see some different jumps I have made, or need some ideas for inspiration, check out my website, or stop by my blog for the latest updates on what I am creating, or how my horse Frisby is keeping me entertained.

http:www.coloradohorsejumps.com

4851257R10041

Printed in Great Britain
by Amazon.co.uk, Ltd.,
Marston Gate.